PEOPLE IN MY NEIGHBORHOOD

THE POSTAL WORKER

Jared Siemens

LIGHTBOX
openlightbox.com

LIGHTBOX

Go to
www.openlightbox.com
and enter this book's
unique code.

ACCESS CODE

LBXR2274

Lightbox is an all-inclusive digital solution for the teaching and learning of curriculum topics in an original, groundbreaking way. Lightbox is based on National Curriculum Standards.

OPTIMIZED FOR
- ✓ **TABLETS**
- ✓ **WHITEBOARDS**
- ✓ **COMPUTERS**
- ✓ **AND MUCH MORE!**

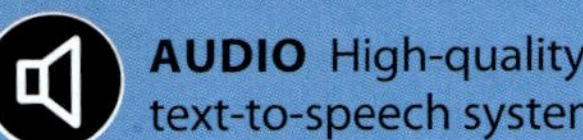

STANDARD FEATURES OF LIGHTBOX

 **AUDIO** High-quality narration using text-to-speech system

 **VIDEOS** Embedded high-definition video clips

 **ACTIVITIES** Printable PDFs that can be emailed and graded

 **WEBLINKS** Curated links to external, child-safe resources

 **SLIDESHOWS** Pictorial overviews of key concepts

 **INTERACTIVE MAPS** Interactive maps and aerial satellite imagery

QUIZ **QUIZZES** Ten multiple choice questions that are automatically graded and emailed for teacher assessment

 **KEY WORDS** Matching key concepts to their definitions

VIDEOS

WEBLINKS

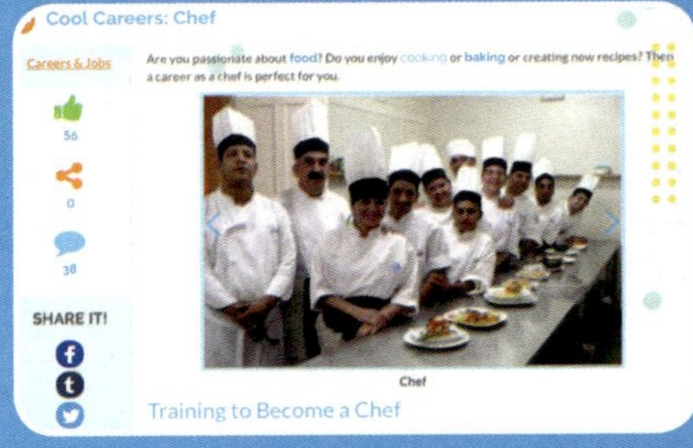

SLIDESHOWS

QUIZZES

PEOPLE IN MY NEIGHBORHOOD

THE POSTAL WORKER

CONTENTS

There are many different people in my neighborhood.

The postal worker is a person in my neighborhood.

Many postal workers start their day at a post office.

The first post office in the United States was founded in **1639**, in **Boston, Massachusetts**.

A post office is a place where mail is gathered and sorted for delivery.

A postal worker sorts the mail into groups. Each group will go to a different place.

He may sort it by hand or get help from a machine. The machine can sort mail very fast.

The postal worker puts the mail on a mail truck. Then, he begins his route.

A route is a map of the places where he will take the mail.

Postal workers walk from home to home and put mail into each mailbox.

They look at the address on each letter to make sure it gets to the right home.

City postal workers may walk **12 miles** (19 kilometers) or more **each day**.

Some postal workers make special deliveries.

They may use a boat to deliver mail to houses along a river.

Other postal workers stay at the post office.

These postal workers weigh packages and sell stamps to customers.

The **smallest** post office in the United States is found in **Ochopee, Florida**.

Postal workers help people who live far away send each other birthday cards.

Postal workers are important people in my neighborhood.

UNITED STATES
POSTAL SERVICE

See what you have learned about the postal worker.

Describe what you see in each of the pictures.

KEY WORDS

Research has shown that as much as 65 percent of all written material published in English is made up of 300 words. These 300 words cannot be taught using pictures or learned by sounding them out. They must be recognized by sight. This book contains 69 common sight words to help young readers improve their reading fluency and comprehension. This book also teaches young readers several important content words, such as proper nouns. These words are paired with pictures to aid in learning and improve understanding.

Page	Sight Words First Appearance
4	are, different, in, many, my, people, there
5	a, is, the
6	at, day, start, their
7	and, first, for, place, states, was, where
8	each, go, groups, into, to, will
9	by, can, from, get, hand, he, help, it, may, or, very
10	has, his, more, on, puts, than, then
11	of, take
12	home, walk
13	city, letter, look, make, miles, right, they
14	some
15	along, houses, river, use
16	other
17	found, these
18	away, far, live, who
20	important

Page	Content Words First Appearance
4	neighborhood
5	person, postal worker
6	post office
7	Boston, delivery, mail, Massachusetts, United States
9	machine
10	mail truck, route, United States Postal Service, vehicles
11	map
12	mailbox
13	address, letter
15	boat
17	customers, Florida, Ochopee, packages, stamps
18	birthday cards

Published by Smartbook Media Inc.
350 5th Avenue, 59th Floor New York, NY 10118
Website: www.openlightbox.com

Library of Congress Control Number: 2018930452

ISBN 978-1-5105-3829-0 (hardcover)
ISBN 978-1-5105-3830-6 (multi-user eBook)

032018
120117

Printed in Brainerd, Minnesota, United States
1 2 3 4 5 6 7 8 9 0 22 21 20 19 18

Project Coordinator: Jared Siemens
Designer: Nick Newton

The publisher acknowledges Alamy, Getty Images, and iStock as its primary image suppliers for this title.